# How Is a Bicycle Made?

Angela Royston

Heinemann Library
Chicago, Illinois

Customer Service   888–454–2279

Visit our website at www.heinemannlibrary.com

Photo research by Melissa Allison and Debra Weatherley
Designed by Jo Hinton-Malivoire and AMR
Printed and bound in China by South China Printing Company

09 08 07 06 05
10 9 8 7 6 5 4 3 2 1

**Library of Congress Cataloging-in-Publication Data**
Royston, Angela.
   How is a bicycle made? / Angela Royston.
       p. cm. -- (How are things made?)
Includes bibliographical references and index.
   ISBN 1-4034-6637-8 (library binding - hardcover) -- ISBN
1-4034-6644-0 (pbk.)  1.  Bicycles--Design and construction--Juvenile
literature. I. Title. II. Series.
TL410.R67 2004
629.227'2--dc22
                              2004019791

**Acknowledgments**
The author and publisher are grateful to the following for permission to reproduce copyright material:
Corbis pp.**15**, **28** (Charles O'Rear); Corbis/Royalty-free p.**14**; George Robinson p.**16**; Getty Images p.**11**; Getty Images/Photodisc p.**10**; Harcourt Education Ltd /Tudor Photography pp.**13**, **17**; Robert Harding Picture Library p.**12** (J Miller); Stockfile pp.**4**, **6**, **7**, **8**, **9**, **20**, **21**, **22**, **23**, **25**, **26**, **27** (Steven Behr); Trek Bicycle Corporation pp. **18**, **19**, **24**, **28**, **29**.

Cover photograph of bicycles reproduced with permission of Harcourt Education Ltd/Tudor Photography.

Every effort has been made to contact copyright holders of any material reproduced in this book. Any omissions will be rectified in subsequent printings if notice is given to the publisher.

Some words are shown in bold, **like this.** You can find out what they mean by looking in the glossary.

# Contents

# What Is in a Bicycle?

Many children enjoy riding bicycles. Bicycles are made of different materials. Each material helps to make the bicycle strong and to work well.

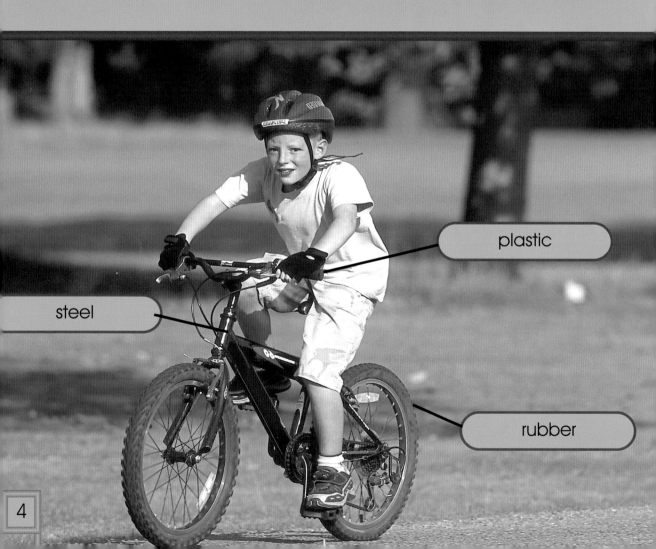

plastic

steel

rubber

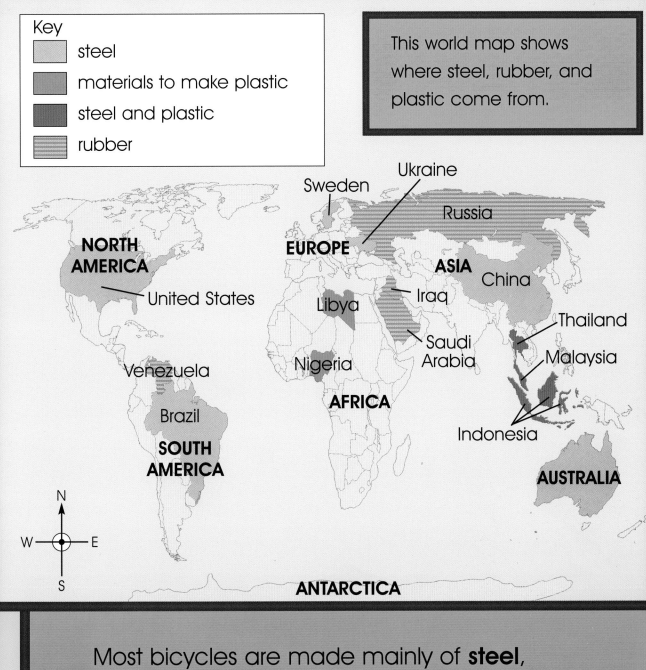

Key
- steel
- materials to make plastic
- steel and plastic
- rubber

This world map shows where steel, rubber, and plastic come from.

Ukraine
Sweden
Russia
NORTH AMERICA
EUROPE
United States
ASIA
China
Libya
Iraq
Thailand
Saudi Arabia
Nigeria
Malaysia
Venezuela
AFRICA
Brazil
Indonesia
SOUTH AMERICA
AUSTRALIA
N
W—E
S
ANTARCTICA

Most bicycles are made mainly of **steel**, **rubber**, and **plastic**. These materials come from many different parts of the world.

5

# Who Makes Bicycles?

Many different **companies** make bicycles. Each company has a factory. Many people work for the company. Workers in the factory make the bicycles.

Some people work in the company's offices. Workers **design** new bicycles. Other workers buy the materials needed to make the bicycles.

# Designing a Bicycle

**Designers** think of new types of bicycles. They draw the **designs** on a computer or on paper. They look for ways to make the bicycles work better.

Experts test bicycles over rough ground.

**Experts** build and test examples of the best bicycles. Then the **company** decides which ones to make and sell.

# Making Steel

The frame of the bicycle is made mainly of **steel**. Steel is made from **iron ore**. Iron ore is dug out of the ground and then it is heated in a **furnace**.

The furnace makes the iron ore so hot it becomes liquid.

Different metals are added to liquid iron to make steel. Steel is stronger than iron. Hot steel is poured into **molds** to make steel tubes.

# Making Rubber Tires

**Rubber** comes from rubber trees. When the bark of a rubber tree is cut, a thick liquid called latex oozes out. The liquid is collected in cups.

This rubber tree in Malaysia has been grown to produce latex.

There are many different sizes of tires.

In the rubber factory, latex is made into rubber. A tire factory buys **bales** of rubber and turns them into tires.

# Where Plastic Comes From

**Plastic** is made from **oil**. Oil is found deep under the ground. Oil workers drill down to reach the oil. The oil is taken to an oil **refinery**.

The oil refinery separates the oil into gasoline and other liquids. Some of the oil is made into plastic.

These small pieces of plastic are made from oil.

# Making the Seat and Fenders

**Plastic** is cheap and can be made into different shapes. Plastic pellets are poured into different-shaped **molds** to make the bicycle seat and the fenders.

Plastic seats are shaped inside a mold.

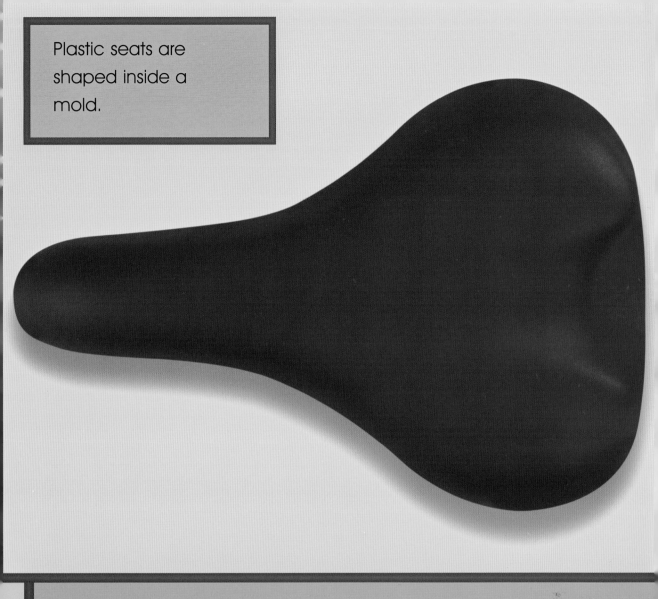

The plastic pellets melt inside the molds and are mixed with a **dye** to color them. When the molds have cooled, they are taken off.

# Making the Frame

Trucks take all the different parts of the bicycle to the bicycle factory. A machine in the factory cuts the **steel** tubes. Another machine bends them into the right shapes.

A worker **welds** the different pieces together to make the frame. This means that the ends of the tubes are heated until they melt together.

The welding light is so bright the worker must wear a mask.

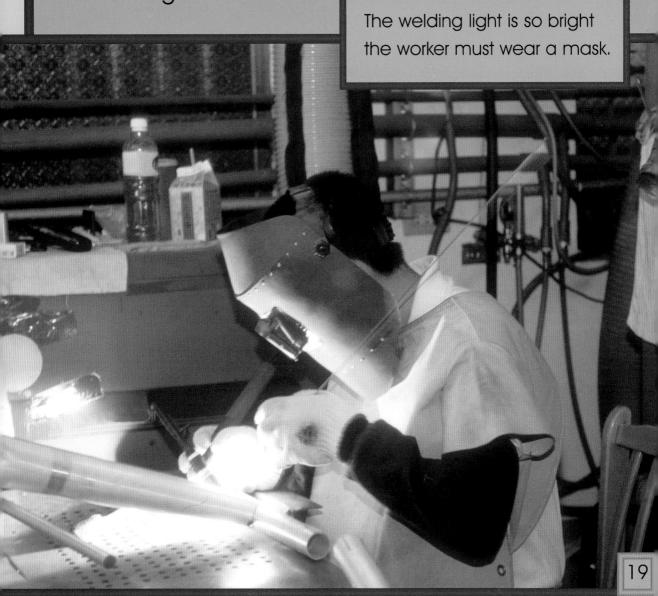

# Making the Wheels

A wheel has a hub, spokes, a rim, and a tire. The spokes are put into the hub. Then a worker fits the spokes into the rim.

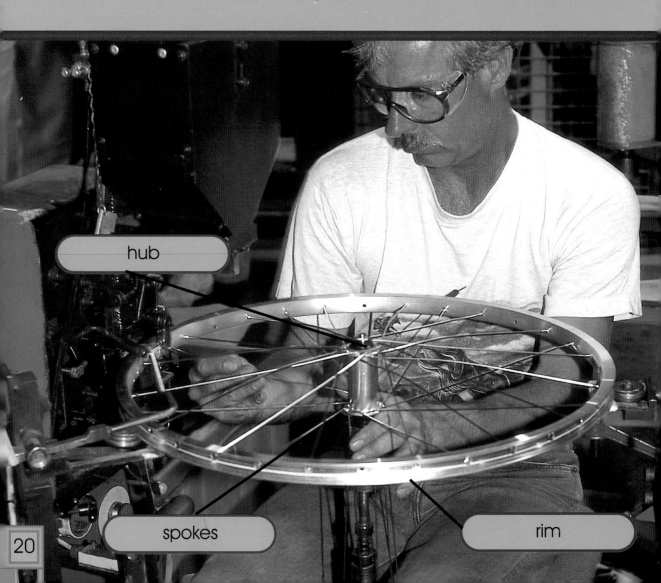

hub

spokes

rim

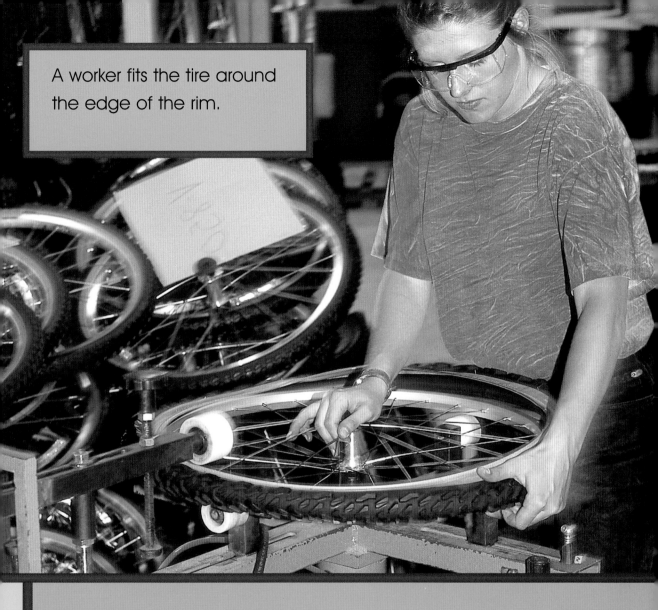

A worker fits the tire around the edge of the rim.

The tire has a thin tube inside called an inner tube. The inner tube is filled with air. The **rubber** and the air make the bike comfortable to ride.

# Putting It All Together

The **steel** frame is sprayed with paint in the paint shop. When the paint is dry, the frame is put onto a **conveyor belt**.

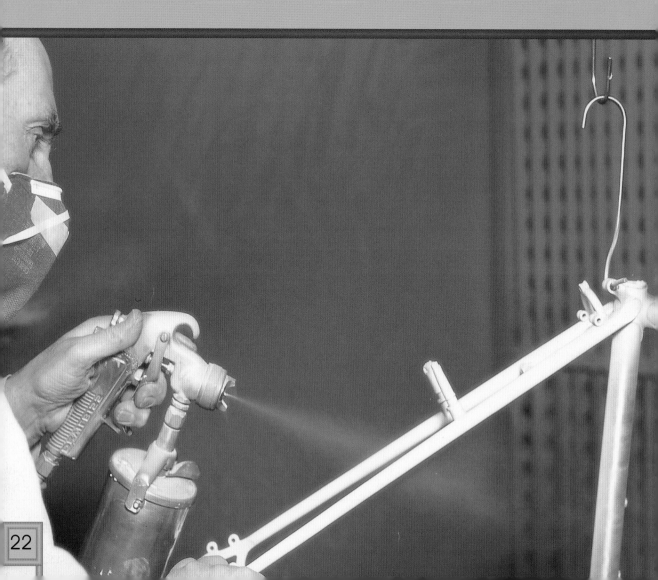

The frame moves along the conveyor belt. Workers and machines add all the parts to the bicycle, one by one.

# The Finished Bicycle

When the bicycle is finished, it is tested to make sure that everything works well. The brakes are tested, as well as the wheels and pedals.

The finished bicycles are stored in a
**warehouse**. When a store needs more
bicycles to sell, the store orders them
from the bicycle **company**.

# Selling the Bicycles

A truck takes the new bicycles from the **warehouse** to different stores. Here people can look at many different bicycles before deciding which one to buy.

Some of the money you pay for a bicycle goes to the bicycle **company**. They use some of this money to make more bicycles.

# From Start to Finish

A bicycle is made mainly of **steel**. Steel is made from **iron ore**.

The steel is made into tubes.

The tubes are bent and joined together to make the frame.

The frame is put on a **conveyor belt**. The other parts are added piece by piece.

# A Closer Look

Every bicycle has the name of the bicycle **company** printed on it. The tires are also printed with the name of the company that made them.

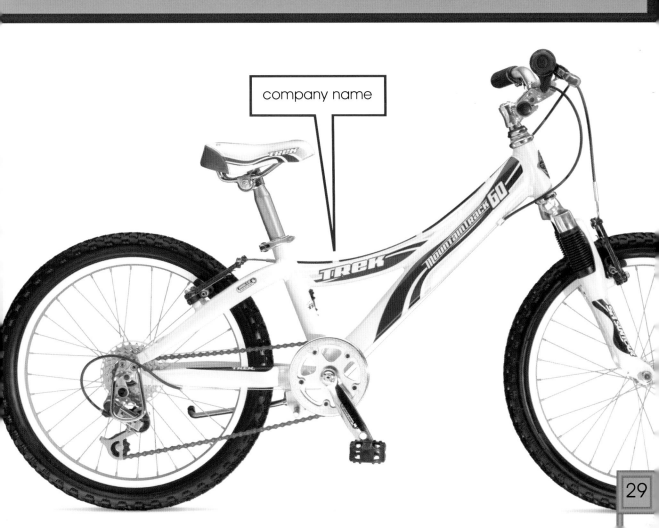

company name

# Glossary

**bale** large amount of something tied up to make a bundle

**company** group of people who work together

**conveyor belt** machine that carries things on a long loop from one place to another

**design** decide how an object or machine will look

**designer** person who decides how an object will look

**dye** substance that gives plastic, paint, or cloth its color

**expert** someone who knows a lot about a topic

**furnace** very hot oven

**iron ore** rock that contains iron

**mold** hollow container

**oil** liquid that forms under the ground

**plastic** material made from oil or coal

**refinery** place where oil is separated into gasoline and other liquids

**rubber** bendy, waterproof material made from the juice of rubber trees

**steel** type of metal made from iron ore

**warehouse** building where things are stored

**welded** joined together by heating the ends of two pieces of metal

# More Books to Read

Cole, Steve and Sarah Rakitin. *Kids Easy Bike Care.*
Charlotte, Vermont: Williamson, 2003.

Englart, Mindy, and Peter Casolino. *Bikes from Start to
Finish*. Woodbridge, Conn.: Blackbirch, 2002.

Pinchuk, Amy, and Tina Holdcroft and Alan Moon. *The
Best Book of Bikes*. Toronto: Firefly, 2003.

# Index

4 5 6 6